Native Americans

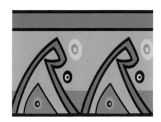

Salinan

Barbara A. Gray-Kanatiiosh

ABDO Publishing Company

visit us at
www.abdopub.com

Published by ABDO Publishing Company, 4940 Viking Drive, Suite 622, Edina, Minnesota 55435. Copyright © 2004 by Abdo Consulting Group, Inc. International copyrights reserved in all countries. No part of this book may be reproduced in any form without written permission from the publisher.

Printed in the United States.

Cover Photo: Corbis
Interior Photos: Corbis pp. 4, 29, 30; Debra Krol p. 27
Illustrations: David Kanietakeron Fadden pp. 7, 9, 11, 13, 15, 17, 19, 21, 23, 25
Editors: Kate A. Conley, Jennifer R. Krueger, Kristin Van Cleaf
Art Direction & Maps: Neil Klinepier

Library of Congress Cataloging-in-Publication Data

Gray-Kanatiiosh, Barbara A., 1963-
   Salinan / Barbara A. Gray-Kanatiiosh.
    p. cm. -- (Native Americans)
   Summary: An introduction to the history, social life and customs, and present status of the Salinan Indians, a tribe whose homelands included valleys, marshes, streams, and shores from Salinas to San Juan Obispo, California.
   Includes bibliographical references and index.
   ISBN 1-57765-937-6
   1. Salinan Indians--History--Juvenile literature. 2. Salinan Indians--Social life and customs--Juvenile literature. [1. Salinan Indians. 2. Indians of North America--California.] I. Title. II. Native Americans (Edina, Minn.)

E99.S17G73 2003
979.4'70049757--dc21
                                           2003051838

About the Author: Barbara A. Gray-Kanatiiosh, JD

Barbara Gray-Kanatiiosh, JD, Ph.D. ABD, is an Akwesasne Mohawk. She resides at the Mohawk Nation and is of the Wolf Clan. She has a Juris Doctorate from Arizona State University, where she was one of the first recipients of ASU's special certificate in Indian Law. Barbara's Ph.D. is in Justice Studies at ASU. She is currently working on her dissertation, which concerns the impacts of environmental injustice on indigenous culture. Barbara works hard to educate children about Native Americans through her writing and Web site, where children may ask questions and receive a written response about the Haudenosaunee culture. The Web site is: www.peace4turtleisland.org

About the Illustrator: David Kanietakeron Fadden

David Kanietakeron Fadden is a member of the Akwesasne Mohawk Wolf Clan. His work has appeared in publications such as *Akwesasne Notes*, *Indian Time*, and the *Northeast Indian Quarterly*. Examples of his work have also appeared in various publications of the Six Nations Indian Museum in Onchiota, NY. His work has also appeared in "How the West Was Lost: Always the Enemy," produced by Gannett Production, which appeared on the Discovery Channel. David's work has been exhibited in Albany, NY; the Lake Placid Center for the Arts; Centre Strathearn in Montreal, Quebec; North Country Community College in Saranac Lake, NY; Paul Smith's College in Paul Smiths, NY; and at the Unison Arts & Learning Center in New Paltz, NY.

Contents

Where They Lived

The Salinan (SAH-lee-nahn) homelands were located in central California, from Salinas in the north to Morro Bay in the south. These lands stretched from the coast of California to the west side of the Central Valley. Neighboring tribes included the Yokut, Ohlone, Esselen, and Chumash.

Big Sur is a coastal region in the traditional Salinan homelands.

The Salinan lived in coastal and inland groups. They lived along rivers such as the Salinas, San Antonio, and Nacimiento. They also lived in valleys, such as the San Antonio Valley. Their territory included the Diablo, Temblor, and the South Coast Ranges. The Salinan also lived along the beaches on the coast of California.

The Salinan lands contained salt marshes, streams, lakes, wetlands, and grasslands. There were also sheer cliffs and rocky beaches. The lands provided homes to many plants and animals. The inlands contained stands of oak trees.

The Salinan language was from the Hokan language family. The Salinan groups spoke different dialects of their language.

Salinan Homelands

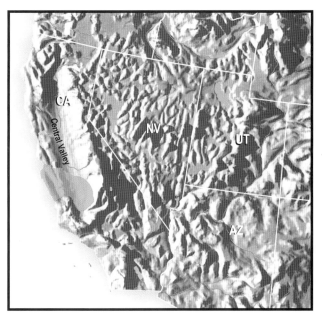

Society

The Salinan were divided into clans with animal **totems**. Bear and Deer were two Salinan clans. Salinan fathers passed their clans on to their children. For example, if a father had Bear as his totem, then his children were also part of Bear clan.

The Salinan clans lived in villages. Each village had a chief. The title of chief belonged to a family. The title was usually passed on from father to son. However, village elders still had to approve new chiefs.

A chief had many responsibilities in his village. He worked hard to keep peace in his village and with neighboring tribes. Salinan chiefs also welcomed visitors and arranged trades.

Chiefs had helpers and messengers. The helpers assisted the chief with arranging hunting, fishing, and gathering trips. Messengers traveled to other villages to announce ceremonies and trips.

Medicine people were also important members of the society. Each medicine person had special healing powers. Some used plants to heal. Others performed ceremonies to bring good weather or good hunting, fishing, and gathering.

A Salinan chief talks to other tribe members.

Food

The Salinan hunted, fished, and gathered their food. They hunted mule deer, elk, and pronghorn with strong, **sinew**-backed bows and arrows.

The Salinan also hunted smaller animals. They hunted squirrels, rabbits, ducks, geese, and otters. They caught these animals in traps, snares, and nets.

Men and women fished in the lakes, rivers, streams, and ponds. They fished for trout, perch, chub, suckers, and salmon. To fish, the Salinan used nets and hook and line. They carved the hooks from shells. Sometimes the Salinan dried the fish in the sun. Other times they baked or broiled the fish.

The Salinan gathered clams, mussels, and other shellfish. They sometimes cooked shellfish over a bed of salt grass or **tule** (TOO-lee) reeds. They also gathered berries and other fruits, wild plants, oats, seeds, tule, and acorns. They roasted the seeds and ground them into flour.

Salinan gather acorns to roast or grind into flour.

Acorns were a staple food for the Salinan. The Salinan had to carefully prepare the acorns to remove the bitter **tannic** acid. Then, they made the prepared acorn flour into mush or soup. They also stored acorns in willow-woven **granaries**. The granary protected the nuts from insects and animals.

The Salinan cooked over fires and in earthen ovens. They also cooked in waterproof baskets. Hot rocks placed into the basket cooked the soup or mush.

Homes

The Salinan built their villages near waterways. There were many villages throughout Salinan territory. They consisted of clusters of dome-shaped homes.

The Salinan built their homes over pits. They built a home's frame with sapling willow poles. They bent the poles and tied them together at the top.

The Salinan strengthened the frame by adding three hoops of different sizes. Then, they covered the frame with **tule** or rye grass mats. They used strips of willow or rope made from plant fibers to tie together the frame, hoops, and mats.

The Salinan also built special houses for their villages. For example, they built **communal** and dance houses. They also built birthing huts. Women went to the birthing hut when a baby was ready to be born.

Villages also had sweathouses. This type of house was built over a deep pit. For that reason, the Salinan needed a ladder to get in and out of the sweathouse. Inside, water was poured over hot rocks, which filled the sweathouse with steam. Sweathouses helped the Salinan to have healthy minds and bodies.

The tops of Salinan homes, covering the pits below

Clothing

In warmer months, the Salinan did not wear much clothing. But sometimes, clothes were necessary. For example, on cold days men and women wore robes woven from rabbit skins. The Salinan made other clothing from grasses, animal skins, furs, and woven feathers.

Men wore **breechcloths** made from rabbit or deerskin. They also sometimes wore **kilts** made from **tule**. Men sometimes wore netting made from feathers and plant fibers. They wore these nets around the waist and used them to carry items.

Women wore aprons. They made these aprons by weaving grass. The back of the apron was usually made of animal skins such as rabbit, deer, or otter. Women also wore bowl-shaped basket hats. They wore these hats while gathering seeds and acorns.

Opposite page: Salinan dressed in traditional clothing

Men and women wore their hair shoulder length and tied it at the neck. They decorated their bodies with paint and permanent tattoos. The Salinan made the tattoos by rubbing charcoal into small cuts.

The Salinan usually went barefoot. When walking on rocky ground, however, they wore sandals or moccasins. Men and women also wore necklaces of shell, bone, and wood beads. They wore earrings and sometimes pierced their noses.

Crafts

The Salinan made beautiful baskets. They made coil, twine, and coarsely woven baskets. They wove these baskets with deer and bunch grass, brake fern, willow, and **tule**.

Their baskets could be used for cooking, gathering, and storing food. The Salinan used large burden baskets to hold nuts and seeds. Burden baskets had a woven strap to help the women carry the baskets on their backs. The women also wove seed-beater baskets. These were used to knock seeds off grasses and into gathering baskets during harvests.

Salinan women also made twined hopper baskets. A hopper basket looked like a funnel with a large hole at the bottom. The Salinan attached a hopper to a stone **mortar** with asphalt. The hopper kept seeds and nut pieces from flying away as they were ground in the mortar.

The Salinan also made gift baskets. They were special baskets decorated with feathers and shells. The people hung strings of shell beads and abalone pieces on them. Sometimes, the baskets also had **geometric** designs.

A Salinan basket weaver practices her craft.

Family

Salinan villages were made up of extended families. Survival of the people depended on each member helping with daily chores. The family moved together to fish, hunt, and gather food. Each member had his or her own special responsibilities.

Women gathered wild plants, seeds, berries, and nuts. The women also dug for purple **amole** lily bulbs under oak trees. These bulbs had many uses. The Salinan could roast the bulbs over a fire and eat them. They could also use the plant to make soap. Men even used the juices of the crushed plant to stun fish.

Men hunted for food. They also wove coarse fishing basket traps. They wove nets and used them with notched stone sinkers to catch fish. They made stone **mortars**, **pestles**, and bowls, too. And, men crafted tools from stone, bone, and shell.

Storytellers also played an important role in Salinan families. Storytellers were important keepers of knowledge. They taught children about their **culture** and history. Elders taught the children about the Salinan dances and songs.

Salinan men used a special method to hunt deer. They walked into a deer herd wearing a disguise made of a deer head and hide. When the men were close enough, they killed a deer with a knife or a bow and arrow.

17

Children

The Salinan carried their babies in cradle baskets. They made these baskets by using the twine method of weaving. The baby slept on a soft **tule** mattress attached to the frame.

As Salinan children grew, they learned useful skills by watching and helping the adults. Girls learned to gather basket-making materials in the wetlands. They gathered tule, willows, and ferns that grew near the water. Girls helped clean and size the basket materials. The women taught the girls how to weave strips of tule into beautiful baskets.

Boys learned how to make small bows and arrows. The arrows had sharpened tips. The boys hunted for small animals with these weapons.

Children also learned how to make musical instruments. They helped to make butterfly cocoon rattles, elderberry clappers, and flutes.

Salinan children had fun playing games, too. They ran, swam, and played hoop and pole. To play this game, the children rolled a small hoop along the ground. The object of the game was to throw the pole through the rolling hoop.

Salinan children learned by listening to the stories of their elders.

Myths

    The Salinan have many stories about Hawk and Raven. This story begins with Hawk and Raven flying in circles in the sky. They had been sent to perform a duty. They needed to make the world safer.

    Near Morro Bay they spotted Taliyekatapelta, the frightful two-headed serpent. Hawk and Raven attacked. They dove from the sky. The two-headed serpent saw the diving birds and began to slither away.

    Hawk and Raven chased the serpent toward Morro Rock. They were told to go to the top of Morro Rock because it is a power spot. The two-headed serpent could only be defeated at this sacred place.

    The serpent wrapped himself around Morro Rock. His two heads reached toward the sky to grab Hawk and Raven. Hawk and Raven became charged with power. They pulled out knives hidden in their wings. They killed the serpent by cutting it into tiny pieces.

Each tiny piece became a black rattlesnake. Today when Salinan elders see a rattlesnake, they tell how Hawk and Raven made the world safer for the people.

Hawk and Raven gain strength at the power spot.

War

The Salinan were a friendly and peace-loving people. They maintained peace with the environment and neighboring tribes. The Salinan economy depended on trade with neighboring tribes.

For example, the Salinan provided shells and shell beads to the Yokut. The Yokut lived north of the Salinan. In exchange for shells, the Salinan received salt grass, **obsidian**, seeds, and tanned hides.

When a conflict arose with other tribes, war was sometimes necessary. In warfare, the Salinan used knives made from obsidian, bone, or antler. They also fought with **sinew**-backed bows.

The Salinan made the bows from cedar. They wrapped the sinew around the bow to make it stronger. Bows were about 48 inches (122 cm) long. The Salinan made bowstrings from twisted plant fibers.

The Salinan used compound arrows. They made the end of the arrow from reed. The Salinan made the front of the arrow from hardwood. They attached an **obsidian** arrowhead to it by using **sinew** and asphalt. Men straightened arrows using a notched stone tool.

A Salinan man uses his bow and compound arrow.

Contact with Europeans

The Salinan welcomed the first Europeans. The Salinan first came into contact with Europeans in the early 1600s. In 1602, Spanish explorer Sebastián Vizcaíno may have met some Salinan who were in **tule** canoes. At this time, there were about 3,000 Salinan living within their homelands.

In the 1770s, Spaniards established three **missions** within Salinan homelands. They built the Mission at Soledad, the Mission San Antonio de Padua, and the Mission San Miguel Arcangel.

Some Salinan were taken from their lands to nearby missions. The Spaniards at the missions forced some of the Salinan to abandon their **cultural** ways. In addition, the Salinan did not have **immunity** to European diseases. Many died from **epidemics**.

However, some Salinan avoided these problems. They lived a blended life. They adapted to the Spaniard's influence, but kept the Salinan language and culture alive.

Until the mid-1800s, the land that includes present-day California belonged to Mexico. When these lands became part of the United States, the Salinan suffered. The Americans enslaved the Salinan. Settlers and gold prospectors killed many Salinan. The Salinan lost people and lands.

Sebastián Vizcaíno meets Salinan in their tule canoes.

Famous Salinan People

The Salinan have had many leaders over the years. When times were bad, these leaders held the people and **culture** together. Today, Salinan leaders are doing the same thing. They are working hard to protect the environment, sacred sites, and culture.

One man who is working hard to protect cultural traditions is Eduardo Jose (Joe) Freeman of the Salinan Natural Cultural Preservation. Freeman's work protects the language and songs of his people. At gatherings, he sings traditional Salinan songs.

Gregg Castro of the Salinan Nation also works to protect Salinan traditions. He works with other council members to restore lands that were stolen from their people years ago.

Debra Krol is another person working to protect Salinan culture. Krol is a journalist and member of the Native American Journalist Association. She uses her gifts in writing and research to bring public attention to issues affecting the Salinan and other California tribes.

Debra Krol

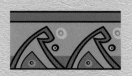# The Salinan Today

There is some confusion about how many Salinan descendants exist today. Some people mistakenly think the Salinan are extinct. However, current estimates show that there are between 700 and 1,500 Salinan descendants. Many of them live within their traditional homelands in the San Antonio Valley.

The Salinan Nation and the Salinan Tribe of Monterey County are working toward becoming **federally recognized**. Federal recognition and a land base would help the Salinan protect their **culture**.

The Salinan are also working to protect the environment and their culture for future generations. Many Salinan are working to protect burial sites and sacred ceremonial sites. They recently fought against the U.S. military testing bombs within their traditional lands.

Today, the Salinan hold gatherings where they sing, dance, and perform ceremonies. The Salinan are working hard to protect the languages and stories of their people. Salinan stories contain traditional teachings and knowledge about the Salinan culture. Passing on stories is just one way the Salinan keep their history and culture alive.

Mission San Antonio was founded in Salinan territory by the Spanish in 1771. The Salinan Nation still meets once a year at the mission.

Carmel Valley (above), part of the traditional Salinan homelands

Point Lobos (left) is a California State Reserve in the heart of Salinan territory. Unlike some of the Salinan's original territory, Point Lobos is protected from development.

Glossary

amole - a part of a plant that can be used as soap.

breechcloth - a piece of hide or cloth, usually worn by men, that wraps between the legs and ties with a belt around the waist.

communal - shared among people who live close together.

culture - the customs, arts, and tools of a nation or people at a certain time.

epidemic - the rapid spread of a disease among many people.

federal recognition - the U.S. government's recognition of a tribe as being an independent nation. The tribe is then eligible for special funding and for protection of its reservation lands.

geometric - made up of straight lines, circles, and other simple shapes.

granary - a storage place for harvested grain.

immunity - protection against diseases.

kilt - a knee-length, skirt-like garment worn by men.

mission - a center or headquarters for religious work.

mortar - a strong bowl or cup in which a material is pounded.

obsidian - a hard rock that is usually glassy and black.

pestle - a club-shaped tool used to pound or crush a substance.

sinew - a band of tough fibers that joins a muscle to another part, such as a bone.

tannic - related to tannin, a bitter tasting yellow or brown mix of chemicals.

totem - an item that serves as a symbol of a particular family or clan.

tule - a type of reed that grows in wetlands. Tule is native to California.

Web Sites

To learn more about the Salinan, visit ABDO Publishing Company on the World Wide Web at **www.abdopub.com**. Web sites about the Salinan are featured on our Book Links page. These links are routinely monitored and updated to provide the most current information available.

Index